CHOCOLATE

50 Easy Recipes

ACADEMIA
BARILLA

CREATED BY
ACADEMIA BARILLA

PHOTOGRAPHY
ALBERTO ROSSI
CHEF MARIO GRAZIA
CHEF LUCA ZANGA

RECIPES
CHEF MARIO GRAZIA

TEXTS
MARIAGRAZIA VILLA

DESIGN
MARINELLA DEBERNARDI

COORDINATION WITH ACADEMIA BARILLA
CHATO MORANDI
ILARIA ROSSI
REBECCA PICKRELL

CONTENTS

CHOCOLATE BLISS

Ah, chocolate. Dark, milk, white. With hints of vanilla, licorice or coffee; flavored with dried fruits and liqueur; combined with pears, strawberries and orange... is there anything more irresistible, more pleasant and comforting? What is it about diving into the goodness of a praline, the exciting crunch of a crispy square, the infinite sweetness of hot chocolate? What is about the sensuousness of mousse, the comforting warmth of hazelnuts, the luxuriousness of caramel, and the simplistic, almost childlike poetry of a mountain of profiteroles?

Not surprisingly, in Central America before Columbus, chocolate's first use was ritualistic, surrounded by an aura of sacredness and mystery. Chocolate, in fact, was only enjoyed by kings, nobles, warriors. It was quickly adopted for use in the kitchen, however, it would never be confused with other foods: it was, according to the Mayans, the "food of the gods". Not surprisingly, it was associated with an almost metaphysical joy, one that was able to lighten and brighten your life.

Not just for sweet confections

From the start, cocoa was not only used to prepare desserts (from the simplest to the most sumptuously extravagant), but also to flavor many savory dishes. In the Italian gastronomic tradition, for example, cocoa was used in dough to create "black pasta", such as tagliatelle, lasagne or pappardelle, which were often paired with white sauces. It was also in used in old regional specialties, such as *cjalsons*, a tortellini dish characteristic of Carnia in the north-eastern region of Friuli, or *pistum*, bittersweet gnocchi made in the same area. It was also used with main course dishes, lending its characteristically bitter and fragrant aromas to numerous game dishes and historical recipes, such as oxtail, typical of Roman cuisine.

A virtuous food – and one to put you in a good mood

Chocolate is a godsend for its nutritional value. Rich in protein (especially milk chocolate), it contains numerous minerals, such as calcium, magnesium, phosphorus, iron, and copper, as well as vitamins A, B1, B2, C, D and E. It also contains valuable flavonoids with a high antioxidant content.

Numerous scientific studies have also highlighted the benefits of chocolate when it comes to wellbeing and mood enhancement. Thanks to the presence of phenylethylamine (a naturally occurring molecule that, when we fall in love, envelops the body in a wave of euphoria), munching on a chocolate bar when you are a bit down can work as an antidepressant.

Everyone is crazy for chocolate

How many famous people have loved chocolate? More than can be counted. Pope Pius V loved it so much that, in 1569, he permitted the consumption of one cup of chocolate a day during periods of fasting. Marie Antoinette, wife of Louis XVI, never went on any journey without her trusted chocolatier... The philosopher Voltaire, in his later years, sipped dozens of cups of chocolate a day to overcome the effects of aging, while seducer extraordinaire Giacomo Casanova followed a similar diet to improve his performance as a lover, confirming the legend of the Aztec god Quetzalcoatl, who was said to have donated the cocoa plant to mortals for its aphrodisiac properties.

Many artists have turned to the muse of chocolate, including numerous writers (such as Goethe and Stendhal) and composers (from Mozart to Strauss). Some, like the children's author Roald Dahl (who used to write with a supply of chocolate at hand), even dedicated a book to his passion: *Charlie and the Chocolate Factory*, which was re-created for the big screen in two hit movies made by Mel Stuart and Tim Burton. The English author Joanne Harris similarly made mouths water with her book *Chocolate*, which was made into the acclaimed film of the same name by Lasse Hallstrom.

Italian desserts and others

The gastronomy of the "food of the gods" owes much to Italy, in particular to the city of Turin. Since the 17th century it has been considered one of the Italian and European capitals of chocolate, and as a result, the region of Piedmont has become known the world over for its great hazelnut paste and spread.

Academia Barilla, an international center dedicated to the preservation and promotion of Italian cuisine, has selected 50 chocolate dessert recipes. These include everything from classic cookies to original desserts, from creams to sweet snacks, from little works of art to the most attractive chocolate cakes. It is not, however, limited to Italian delights, such as Cuneesi al rum, Parmigiani maraschino or Chocolate cannoli. Cocoa, after all, has conquered the world, bringing many excellent recipes into being.

Academia Barilla's selections are varied and comprehensive, focusing on recipes that best exemplify the happy harmony between tradition and innovation, skill and execution, and, above all, the convivial spirit of sharing, or the pleasure of "living with", as the Latin etymology – *convivium* – has it. After all, what better way is there to express joy and comfort with yourself, your family, and your friends than with a smile from a chocolate-covered face?

CHOCOLATE, "FOOD OF THE GODS"

What would life be like if there were no chocolate? It's hard to imagine. It's even harder to imagine the endless colors, shapes, and intensities that chocolate can assume: dark, black, milk, white; in bars, as candy, ice cream, pudding, or cream.

With this ability to adapt, chocolate and the desserts prepared with it are suitable for all occasions: it can be enjoyed in perfect solitude, offered to guests, or given as a gift.

The cacao tree, *Theobroma cacao*, was christened by the naturalist Linnaeus, who chose for it the Greek word *theobroma*, meaning "food of the gods." From it we get chocolate, which is a complete food: it contains fat (45-52%), protein (18-20%), starches, sugars, and minerals. Of particular importance, however, is the presence of theobromine, caffeine, and tannin, which give cocoa therapeutic and medicinal properties.

The legend of chocolate

The history of chocolate goes back a long way. The first to cultivate the cocoa plant in Central America were the Mayans, around 1000 BC, and later, the Aztecs. Legend has it that Quetzalcoatl, Meso-American god, bestowed the cocoa seed – which he used to prepare a bitter, spicy drink with extraordinary energizing and aphrodisiac qualities – on mortals. In his honor, this seed was first called *cacahuatl* and then *xocolatl* (literally "bitter water"). The name would remain similar in almost all languages of the world.

The legend then gives way to history. In 1502, during his fourth and last voyage to the Indies, Christopher Columbus arrived in Honduras, where he was offered a beverage made from the cocoa bean. The taste of chocolate in those days, however, was not particularly pleasant to Europeans, and Columbus did not give it much importance.

Seventeen years later, in 1519, Hernán Cortés arrived from Spain to conquer the New World. He was promptly mistaken for the god Quetzalcoatl, who, according to legend, was supposed to return that year. For this reason, he was peacefully welcomed by Emperor Montezuma.

Cortés was offered a cocoa plantation, the grains of which had monetary value for the Aztecs. Cortés immediately realized the economic value of cocoa and took it to Spain. Back in the old country, friars began replacing the pepper and chili, with which the Aztecs flavored their foamy chocolate, with sugar and vanilla, creating a sweet and tasty drink. This simple adjustment made all the difference for the European palette, and, for most of the 16th century, Cortés' discovery was considered a great "deal" for the Spanish court.

Chocolate in Europe

For a time, Charles V (1500-1558) and the Spanish court were the center from which the knowledge of chocolate radiated to all the courts of Europe. However, it was during the reign of Philip II (1527-1598), who loved chocolate, that its use spread among the wealthy bourgeoisie, and later, among all social classes. Cocoa consumption was so high that large, and lucrative, smuggling operations by the British and Dutch developed. Cocoa at that time only came from Mexico, though it would soon also be brought from Venezuela and the island of Trinidad.
The first appearance of cocoa in France was recorded in 1612. It seems to have been introduced by Alphonse de Richelieu, Cardinal-Archbishop of Lyon, and brother of the Louis XIII's celebrated minister. He had learned about it from an Italian in Spain, and had started to use it medicinally, as he considered it effective for moderating the "vapors of the spleen," from which he suffered. Cardinal Mazarin, who became prime minister in 1642, was said to be so greedy for it, he brought over a famous *chocolatier*, a man named More, from Italy. Later, Napoleon prized chocolate as an energy booster, and he often offered chocolate (along with large sums of money) to his generals as a reward. In his short reign, Napoleon III urged the development of French industry and one that benefited from his influence was that of chocolate. From 1855 to 1870, the French chocolate industry was the most famous in the world.

Chocolate in Italy

In Italy, the fashion of drinking chocolate was imported from Madrid by Duke Emanuele Filiberto of Savoy (1528-1580), general of the Spanish armies directly under the Emperor Charles V. Its popularity, however, had to wait for an illustrious marriage – that between Catherine, daughter of Philip II of Spain, and Duke Carlo Emanuele I, son of Emanuele Filiberto, celebrated in 1587; this overcame the distrust of the new beverage and thereafter chocolate quickly won over the Italian nobility.
By the 17th century the chocolate makers of Venice, Florence, and especially Turin, had become great experts in the art of preparing cocoa, and were exporting products throughout Europe. The first document on the production of chocolate in Italy, kept at the State Archives of Turin, dates back to 1678. Piedmont chocolatiers, however, soon made their mark, matching chocolate with other regional products, such as hazelnuts and chestnuts, to create exciting new recipes. In the same century, knowledge of cocoa spread to Naples and Milan, the vice-royalties of Spain in Italy. In the century that followed, the consumption of chocolate became even more common, becoming something often shared in company.

From a chocolate beverage to chocolate

At the end of the 18th century, the "solid" preparation that we now associate with the word "chocolate" did not exist.

It was in 1828 that the Dutch chemist Coenraad J. Van Houten invented a press to squeeze cocoa butter from cocoa beans, obtaining a cocoa "cake"; this was further processed into powdered form and the fat was removed (this was very similar to the cocoa powder of the present day). The invention quickly spread to Britain and Italy.

Chocolatiers in Switzerland and Turin were also instrumental in the development of processes that "solidified" chocolate into the numerous forms we know today. In the early 19th century, artisans from all over Europe came to Turin to refine and develop this art. Among these, Caffarel and Prochet were the biggest names of the first generation of industrial confectioners, heirs to an ancient tradition associated with the Waldensian migration from France. Many Waldensians, in fact, had fled persecution and settled in Piedmont, and more specifically, the chocolate trade, in which they would play a large role. It was no coincidence that another big name in the nascent confectionery industry was also of Waldensian origin: Michele Talmone.

For a time, then, the confectioneries of Turin were the industry's de facto educational system, pulling in students and apprentices from all over Europe and producing experienced *chocolatiers* who would go on to develop the industry further. An example was François Louis Cailler who, having worked in Turin, went back to Switzerland in 1819 and founded a factory in Corsier, on Lake Geneva. Cailler cleverly used the condensed milk produced by Henri Nestlé to produce milk chocolate in 1875. It has also been said that Philippe Suchard "interned" in Turin in 1826. He would be instrumental in developing the Swiss chocolate industry, which was to become one of the largest in the world.

With these passionate *chocolatiers* and their important technical developments, the industry thrived, turning the '"food of the gods" into a treat for all.

The "chocolate tree"

Chocolate's botanical name is *Theobroma cacao* and it is grown on plantations on a narrow band of land between 20° North and 20° South of the equator. At that latitude the ideal altitude is about 13,000 feet (400 meters), and the temperature must remain constant between 68 and 86 °F (20 and 30 °C), never dropping below 61 °F (16 °C). The ideal habitat is the rain forest, with its ample supply of flies responsible for pollination (a

particular type of fly is required for this). Cocoa trees begin to bear fruit only after 4 to 5 years and they are active for up to 60 years. The beans, or seeds, are housed in egg-shaped fruits called pods, which grow from the trunk or main branches, and are shaped like a rugby ball. When mature, they have a characteristic yellow ochre color. Harvesting takes place twice a year and the fruits are cut in half with a machete.
The interior of the cocoa beans are wrapped in a white spongy pulp. After harvesting, the seeds are put to ferment with the pulp, until they acquire a pink color and a distinctive flavor. They are then set out to dry in the sun. Only then do they take on a definitive "chocolate" color.
A plant produces on average 2 1/4 to 4 1/2 lb (1 to 2 kg) of seeds a year, but during the drying phase, the beans lose about 50% of their weight. The are two main varieties: Forastero, which are tough and productive (80% of the global harvest comes from these plants); and Criollo, which are of a superior quality and flavor, and are often used in a blend with Forastero.

From cocoa to chocolate processing

The process by which cocoa beans become chocolate is a long and complex one. Every manufacturer works the beans according to a closely guarded formula. The individual stages of processing, however, are generally the same throughout the world. It begins with the roasting of the beans, allowing the aroma to develop. The beans are then shelled and peeled. The grains obtained, called nibs, are then milled to get cocoa butter and a fluid paste, cocoa paste; once cooled, this hardens and forms bitter chocolate. If the fluid paste is further pressed, the result is more cocoa butter and a solid residue, that, once milled, becomes cocoa powder. In this phase, cocoa butter, sugar, and flavorings (such as vanilla) are added to produce sweet chocolate.
Milk chocolate was originally obtained in 1876 with condensed milk. Today it is produced with milk powder.
We owe the velvety quality of chocolate to a brilliant Swiss named Rodolphe Lindt, who came up with the invention of "conching." Up to 1880, chocolate had a granular taste that was a bit harsh. Lindt increased the percentage of cocoa butter and, using machinery he developed himself, he mixed the chocolate continuously for days on end, very much longer than usual. The result of this innovation was the creamy, thick and velvety chocolate we all love today.

Giancarlo Gonizzi
*Curator of the **Academia Barilla Gastronomic Library***

Your Own Personal Patisserie

LADY'S KISSES (BACI DI DAMA)

INGREDIENTS FOR 4 PEOPLE

1 cup (125 g) all-purpose flour
5/8 cup (125 g) sugar
3/4 cup (100 g) roasted hazelnuts
scant 1/4 cup (25 g) blanched almonds
generous 1/2 cup (125 g) butter
3/8 cup (30 g) cocoa powder
3 1/2 oz (100 g) dark chocolate

METHOD

Finely grind the hazelnuts and almonds with the sugar in a blender, using the pulse feature. In a bowl, mix the resulting powder with the butter, softened at room temperature.
Sift the flour and cocoa powder together, then incorporate into the mixture, stirring it as little as possible. Wrap the mixture in plastic wrap and leave in the refrigerator for at least 30 minutes.
After this, roll out the mixture with a rolling pin on a lightly floured pastry board to a thickness of about 3/8 in (1 cm). Cut out discs with pastry rings 5/8 to 3/4 cm (1.5 to 2 cm) in diameter and shape into balls with your hands (using this technique, they will all be the same weight).
Arrange the balls on a lightly buttered, floured baking sheet (or one lined with parchment paper) and bake in the oven at 325 °F (160 °C) for about 15 minutes.
Leave to cool completely, then remove them from the pan and turn them upside-down.
Meanwhile, melt the chocolate in a bain-marie or microwave. Let it cool and when it starts to crystallize, pour a little on each of half the total number of baci di dama. Place another one on top of each of the baci and leave to set.

Preparation time: 40' Resting time: 30'
Cooking time: 15' Difficulty: medium

COOKIES WITH CHOCOLATE CHIPS

INGREDIENTS FOR 4 PEOPLE

generous 1 1/2 cups (200 g) all-purpose flour
1 cup (180 g) chocolate chips
1/2 cup (100 g) sugar
3/8 cup (90 g) butter
1 egg
1 tsp (3 g) baking powder
vanilla powder
salt

METHOD

In a bowl, cream the butter, softened at room temperature, with the sugar, then incorporate a pinch of salt and the egg. Sift the flour with baking powder and a pinch of vanilla powder. Add to the mixture, then knead with your hands until the dough is smooth. Finally, stir in the chocolate chips. On a floured surface, use the resulting mixture to form a length about 1 in (2.5 cm) in diameter. Cut into pieces and form into balls with your hands. Line a baking sheet with parchment paper and arrange the balls, spaced at least 1 in (2.5 cm) apart. Flatten each ball slightly with the palm of your hand so that they will take on the traditional cookie shape. Bake in the oven at 350 °F (180 °C) for about 15 minutes.

Preparation time 20'
Cooking time: 15' Difficulty: easy

CHOCOLATE HAZELNUT BISCUITS

INGREDIENTS FOR 4 PEOPLE

1 cup (125 g) confectioners' (powdered) sugar
1/4 cup (25 g) cocoa powder
1 egg white
generous 1/2 cup (75 g) chopped, toasted hazelnuts
2 tbsp (15 g) potato starch
1 tsp (3 g) baking powder
vanilla powder

METHOD

On a pastry board, sift together the confectioners' (powdered) sugar, cocoa, starch, baking powder, and a pinch of vanilla powder. Mix with the egg white and as soon as the mixture becomes smooth, add the chopped toasted hazelnuts.
Lightly flour the pastry board, then form the mixture into a length about 1 1/4 in (3 cm) in diameter. Cut into slices 3/8 in (1 cm) thick. Arrange the biscuits on a lightly buttered, floured baking sheet (or one lined with parchment paper) and bake at 340 °F (170 °C) for 10 to 12 minutes.
Leave to cool completely before removing from the pan.

Preparation time: 20'
Cooking time: 10-12' Difficulty: easy

CHOCOLATE "S" COOKIES

INGREDIENTS FOR 4 PEOPLE

For the "S" shaped cookies
1 1/4 cups (165 g) all-purpose flour
1/3 cup (75 g) of confectioners' (powdered) sugar
1/4 cup (25 g) cocoa powder
scant 1/2 cup (100 g) butter
1 egg
vanilla powder
salt

For the glaze
7 oz (200 g) dark chocolate

METHOD

On a pastry board, sift together the flour, sugar, cocoa powder, and a pinch of vanilla powder. Mix with softened butter and a pinch of salt, so as to obtain a powdery mixture. Stir in the egg, mixing until you have an even dough. Wrap the dough in plastic wrap and leave to rest in the refrigerator for at least an hour.
After this, use a piping bag with a metal tip form a long strand about 3/8 in (1 cm) in diameter (like a long breadstick) on a floured pastry board. Cut into pieces, each about 2 1/2 to 3 in (6 to 7 cm) long, and place on a lightly buttered, floured baking sheet, bending them into the shape of a capital S.
Bake at 350 °F (180 °C) for 13 to 15 minutes.
Leave to cool completely, then remove from the pan.
To prepare the tempered dark chocolate: melt the chocolate in a bain-marie or microwave at 115–120 °F (45–50° C) (use a cooking thermometer), then pour one-third to one-half onto a marble surface. Let this cool until it reaches 80 °F (26–27 °C), then add it on top of the remaining hot chocolate. When the temperature of this new mixture reaches 90 °F (31–32° C), it is ready to be used.
Soak half of the "S" cookies in this tempered chocolate. Let them drain and put them to dry. Wait until the chocolate has solidified. Serve.

Preparation time: 40' Resting time: 1 h
Cooking time: 13-15' Difficulty: medium

SHORTBREAD COOKIES WITH COCOA BEANS

INGREDIENTS FOR 4 PEOPLE

5/8 cup (140 g) butter
1/3 cup (65 g) sugar
20 g (1/4 cup) cocoa powder
1 2/3 cups (190 g) all-purpose flour
1 egg
5 tbsp (25 g) crushed cocoa beans
vanilla powder
salt

METHOD

Cut the butter into cubes, put them in a bowl, then leave to soften at room temperature. Now add the sugar, flour, cocoa, a pinch of salt, and vanilla powder. Sift, working with your fingertips until you have a sandy mixture, then add the egg yolk (keep the egg white for use later in the recipe). Knead just enough to form a smooth, even dough.
Wrap with plastic wrap and place in the refrigerator for 30 minutes.
Remove the dough and put it on a lightly floured work surface.
Form a round length about 1 1/4 in (3 cm) in diameter.
Put in the refrigerator for another 30 minutes.
Remove the dough from the refrigerator, brush it with the egg white (lightly beaten with a fork), and roll it in crushed cocoa beans, making sure they adhere well.
Cut the length of dough into slices about 3/8in (1 cm) thick and place these biscuits on a baking tray lined with parchment paper.
Bake at 375 °F (190°C) for about 13 minutes.

Preparation time: 15' Resting time: 1 h
Cooking time: 13' Difficulty: easy

CHOCOLATE MERINGUES

INGREDIENTS FOR 4 PEOPLE

3 1/2 oz (100 g) egg whites
1 cup (200 g) sugar
1/4 cup (25 g) cocoa powder

METHOD

Start whisking the egg whites in a large bowl. When they start to stiffen in the middle, incorporate a quarter of the sugar and continue beating the eggs until you have a firm, snow-like substance.
Add the remaining sugar mixed with cocoa, folding it in gently with a spatula from top to bottom (so that the mixture does not separate).
Form the meringues into desired shapes on a pan lined with parchment paper, using a piping bag (for example, to obtain a mushroom shape, form the heads and stems separately and join them together after cooking).
Sprinkle the meringues with cocoa powder and cook in the oven at 210 °F (100 °C) for about 2 hours, or until they are dry.
If possible, leave the oven door slightly open so as to allow the moisture to escape.
The meringues will keep for a long time, provided they are kept away from moisture (for example, in a glass jar with an airtight seal).

Preparation time: 30'
Cooking time: 2 h Difficulty: easy

CHOCOLATE BULL'S-EYES

INGREDIENTS FOR **12** BULL'S-EYES

For the chocolate shortbread
1 1/4 cups (165 g) all-purpose flour
3/8 cup (95 g) butter
generous 3/8 cup (85 g) sugar
2 egg yolks
1/4 tsp (1 g) baking powder (optional)
7 tsp (9 g) cocoa powder
vanilla powder
salt

For the filling
2 tbsp (30 g) orange marmalade

For the ganache
2 oz (60 g) dark chocolate
4 tbsp (60 ml) cream
1 tsp (6 ml) glucose syrup

METHOD

In a bowl, mix the softened butter with the sugar, stirring in a pinch of salt and the egg yolks.
Add flour sifted with baking powder (optional), a hint of vanilla, and cocoa powder, then knead briefly until you have a smooth dough.
Wrap the dough in plastic wrap and leave to rest in refrigerator for at least an hour.
After this, work the dough with a rolling pin on a lightly floured work surface until it is about a little under 1/4 in (4-5 mm) thick. Cut out discs using pastry rings 2 in (5 cm) in diameter, allowing two disks for each bull's-eye.
Divide the bull's-eyes equally between two lightly greased and floured baking sheets (or two baking sheets lined with parchment paper).
Using a pastry ring 1 1/2 in (4 cm) in diameter, make a hole in the center of the disks on the first pan.
Bake at 350 °F (180 °C) for 12 to 13 minutes, removing the disks with holes (the "rings") a couple of minutes earlier than the other pan.
Let the rings and disks cool completely.
Turn the disks over and spread them with orange marmalade.
Cover these disks with the rings (the marmalade will ensure that they adhere).
For the ganache, chop the chocolate and place in a bowl. In a small saucepan, bring the cream to the boil with the glucose syrup. Pour the hot mixture over the chocolate. Mix thoroughly with a soft spatula (do not use a whisk since it would incorporates too much air, which will lead to bubbles) until you have smooth, velvety cream.
Fill the cavity of the bull's-eyes with the ganache, using a piping bag.

Preparation time: 40' + 20' (chocolate shortbread)
Cooking time: 13-15' Resting time: 1 h Difficulty: medium

CHOCOLATE TUILES

INGREDIENTS FOR 4 PEOPLE

For the tuiles
5/8 cup (125 g) cane sugar
2 tbsp (28 ml) glucose syrup
1 tbsp (15 ml) water
1/4 cup (65 g) butter
generous 3/4 cup (90 g) slivered almonds
1/2 cup (65 g) all-purpose flour
5 tbsp (25 g) crushed cocoa beans
salt

For the glaze
7 oz (200 g) dark chocolate

METHOD

In a small saucepan, melt the sugar and glucose syrup, water, and butter. Add a pinch of salt and the slivered almonds, then mix together. Finally, add the sifted flour and the crushed cocoa beans. Pour into a bowl, cover with plastic wrap, and leave to rest overnight. Shape into balls about the size of half a walnut and place them 4 in (10 cm) apart on a baking sheet lined with parchment paper. Bake at 325 °F (160 °C) for about 20 minutes. When they are ready, let them cool slightly for just a few moments, then shape them, using a rolling pin or a bottle. To prepare the tempered dark chocolate: melt the chocolate in a bain-marie or microwave at 113–122 °F (45–50° C) (use a cooking thermometer), then pour one-third to one-half onto a marble surface. Let this cool until it reaches 79–81 °F (26–27 °C), then add it on top of the remaining hot chocolate. When the temperature of this new mixture reaches 88–90 °F (31–32° C), it is ready to be used. Once cool, dip half of each tuile in the tempered chocolate. Let them drain and dry. Wait until the chocolate has solidified before serving. Store them in a dry, cool place.

Preparation time: 15' Resting time: 12 h
Cooking time: 20' Difficulty: easy

Chocolate Delights

CHILI PEPPER CHOCOLATE IN CUPS

INGREDIENTS FOR 4 PEOPLE

For the chocolate

2 cups (500 ml) milk
3/8 cup (100 ml) cream
1/2 cup (100 g) sugar
3 1/2 oz (100 g) dark chocolate
1/4 cup (25 g) cocoa powder
4 tsp (10 g) cornstarch (cornflour)
chili pepper

For the decoration

7 oz (200 g) sweetened whipped cream

METHOD

Mix the sugar with the cocoa, cornstarch, and a pinch of chili pepper. Pour the milk and cream into a saucepan and heat over low heat. Pour in the prepared mixture and bring to a boil, stirring with a whisk. Remove from the heat and adjust the amount of chili if necessary. Pour the chocolate into cups and dip a bar of dark chocolate into it, so that it melts slowly.
Garnish each cup with a little sweetened whipped cream (to taste).

Preparation time: 5'
Cooking time; 10' Difficulty: easy

CHOCOLATE CREPES

INGREDIENTS FOR 4 PEOPLE

For the crepes
1 cup (120 g) all-purpose flour
2 eggs
3 1/2 tbsp (40 g) sugar
1/4 cup (20 g) cocoa powder
1 cup (250 ml) milk
3 1/2 tbsp (50 g) butter
salt

For the chocolate pastry cream
4 egg yolks
3/4 cup (150 g) sugar
1/3 cup (40 g) all-purpose flour
2 cups (500 ml) milk
a vanilla bean
3/8 cup (30 g) cocoa powder
3 oz (75 g) dark chocolate, finely chopped

For the decoration scant 1/2 cup (30 g) grated coconut

METHOD

Sift the flour with the cocoa and place in a bowl with the eggs, sugar, and salt. Add in the milk, stirring with a whisk. Then add half the melted butter. Cover and leave the batter to rest in the refrigerator for an hour.
For the chocolate pastry cream, warm the milk in a saucepan with the vanilla bean (cut open lengthwise with a paring knife). Meanwhile, whisk the egg yolks and sugar in a bowl, then add the sifted flour and mix well. Remove the vanilla bean from the milk.
Pour a little boiling milk on the eggs, then gradually add the rest of the milk to temper them, whisking all the time.
Put the mixture back into the saucepan and bring to the boil. Dissolve the cocoa and the chopped dark chocolate in the hot cream. Pour the cream into a suitable container and leave to cool.
Remove the batter from the refrigerator, stir well, and start making the crepes. Pour a ladleful onto a crepe pan or skillet, greased with some of the remaining butter and brought to a high heat. Try to get as thin a film as possible.
As soon as the crepe start to color, flip it and cook on the other side. Stuff each crepe with the chocolate pastry cream, fold into quarters and place on an ovenproof dish. Bake at 340 °F (170 °C) for 5 minutes, then remove from the oven and sprinkle with grated coconut.

Preparation time: 30' + 25' (chocolate pastry cream)
Resting time: 1 h Cooking time: 5' Difficulty: medium

CHOCOLATE FONDUE

INGREDIENTS FOR 4 PEOPLE

For the fondue
1 lb 5 oz (600 g) dark chocolate
Light olive oil (if necessary)

For the fruit
2 bananas
10 oz (300 g) strawberries
2 kiwifruit

METHOD

Melt the chocolate on a low heat.
If it is too thick, dilute it by adding extra virgin olive oil until you have the desired density.
Wash the strawberries. Peel the bananas and the kiwifruit.
Cut the fruit into pieces and thread them onto wooden skewers, which you and your guests can then use to dip in the chocolate fondue.

Preparation time: 15'
Difficulty: easy

CHOCOLATE ICE CREAM

INGREDIENTS FOR ABOUT 4 CUPS (900 ML) OF ICE CREAM

2 cups (500 ml) milk
5/8 cup (130 g) sugar
scant 5/8 cup (50 g) cocoa powder
1/2 oz (15 g) dextrose
1/8 oz (3.5 g) stabilizer
1/3 oz (10 g) dark chocolate

METHOD

In a saucepan bring the milk to 115 °F (45° C).
Mix the sugar, dextrose, stabilizer, and cocoa together, then pour in the milk.
Heat to 159 °F (65 °C) and pasteurize at 185 °F (85° C). Add the dark chocolate.
Put the mixture in a container immersed in a basin of water and ice and quickly cool to 39 °F (4° C).
Leave to 'ripen' at 40 °F (4° C) for 6 hours, then freeze it using an ice cream maker until the mixture is foamy and dry in appearance, that is, not shiny (the time needed depends on the ice cream maker used).

Preparation time: 20' Ripening time: 6 h
Difficulty: medium

CHOCOLATE GRANITA (SLUSH)

INGREDIENTS FOR 4 PEOPLE

1/4 cup (25 g) cocoa powder
1 1/2 cups (400 ml) water
generous 3/8 cup (80 g) sugar

METHOD

Boil the water. Mix the cocoa and sugar together, then pour it into the boiling water, stirring with a whisk. Leave the mixture to cool, then put it in a bowl and place it in the freezer. Stir the granita with a whisk from time to time, breaking up the pieces as they begin to freeze.
Continue in this way, until the whole is transformed into a even granita. Remove from the freezer and serve in four individual bowls.

Preparation time: 2 h
Difficulty: easy

CHOCOLATE SEMIFREDDO

INGREDIENTS FOR 4 PEOPLE

12 oz (325 g) semi-whipped cream

For the chocolate pastry cream

2 egg yolks
3/8 cup (75 g) sugar
3 tbsp (20 g) all-purpose flour
1 cup (250 ml) milk
1/4 vanilla bean
3 tbsp (15 g) cocoa powder

1 1/2 oz (40 g) dark chocolate, chopped

For the Italian meringue

2 oz (60 g) egg whites
5/8 cup (120 g) sugar
4 tsp (20 ml) water

For the dough (chocolate rolls)

1/2 cup (100 g) sugar
3 eggs
1 egg yolk
2/3 cup (80 g) all-purpose flour
2 1/2 tbsp (20 g) potato starch
3 tbsp (15 g) cocoa

For the syrup (the minimum quantity for good results)

2 tbsp (30 ml) water
3/8 cup (80 g) sugar
2 tbsp (35 ml) rum (or other liqueur to taste)

METHOD

For the chocolate roll dough, sift together the flour, starch, and cocoa. Separate the eggs, then beat the egg whites and sugar together in a bowl until stiff. Break the egg yolks into another bowl, beat with a fork, fold in the stiffened egg whites, then add the sifted flour and cocoa with starch. Spread the dough in a layer about 3/8 in (1 cm) thick on a baking sheet lined with parchment paper. Bake at 450 °F (230° C) for 5 to 7 minutes.
Place a layer of dough on the bottom of the molds, then add 3 tbsp (50 ml) syrup (prepared by boiling the sugar and water together, leaving it to cool, then adding the rum).
For the cream, heat the milk in a saucepan with half a vanilla bean (cut open lengthways with a small knife).
Beat the egg yolks and sugar in a bowl, then add the sifted flour and mix well. Remove the vanilla bean from the milk. Pour a little boiling milk on the eggs, then gradually add the rest of the milk to temper them, whisking all the time. Put in a saucepan and bring to the boil. Dissolve the cocoa and chopped dark chocolate in the hot cream. Pour into a bowl and leave to cool.
For the meringue, heat 1/2 cup (105 g) sugar with 4 tsp (20 ml) water, bringing it to 250 °F (121 °C). Beat 2 oz (60 g) egg whites with 5 tsp (15 g) sugar. When the egg mixture has stiffened, the sugar will have cooked: keep beating the eggs, however, until everything is lukewarm.
Add 3 1/2 oz (100 g) meringue to 10 oz (275 g) pastry cream and lighten with the semi-whipped cream, incorporating it gently. Fill the molds and freeze. Remove from the molds 15 minutes before serving and decorate as desired.

Preparation time: 1 h + 25' (pastry cream) + 25' (dough for the chocolate rolls) + 10' (syrup)
Freezing: 3 h Difficulty: hard

Luxurious Creams by the Spoonful

CHOCOLATE AND MINT GLASSES

INGREDIENTS FOR 4 PEOPLE

1 cup (250 ml) cream
1 cup (250 ml) milk
3/4 cup (150 g) sugar
1 oz (25 g) dark chocolate, chopped
1/4 oz (7 g) leaf gelatin
1 tsp (5 ml) peppermint essence
a few drops of green food coloring

METHOD

Boil the milk and cream with the sugar.
Add the gelatin, previously soaked and squeezed, and let it dissolve. Divide this panna cotta mixture into three parts. Leave the first neutral. Flavor the second with the peppermint essence and color it with a few drops of green food coloring. Enrich the last one with the chocolate. Strain a layer of the first cream into four cups and let it stand in the refrigerator to thicken. Then pour in a layer of the next cream and let it thicken (if it had become too thick to pour, heat it gently to make it liquid). Finally add the last, colored panna cotta.
Keep the glasses in the refrigerator until ready to serve.

Preparation time: 30' Cooling time: 2 h
Difficulty: easy

BONET

INGREDIENTS FOR 4/6 PEOPLE

For the bonet

1 1/2 cups (375 ml) milk
3 eggs
generous 1/2 cup (115 g) sugar
1/4 cup (25 g) cocoa powder
1 tsp (5 ml) rum
3 oz (75 g) macaroons (amaretti)

For the caramel

1/2 cup (100 g) sugar
2 tbsp (25 ml) water

METHOD

In a pan, caramelize the sugar with water until it turns a deep blonde color, then pour it into the bottom of a mold or individual molds and leave to cool.
In another saucepan, boil the milk.
Meanwhile, whisk the eggs and sugar together in a bowl, then add the cocoa, amaretti crumbs, and rum.
Add the boiling milk, stir, and pour into the previously caramelized molds.
Bake in a bain-marie at 300–325 °F (150–160 °C) for about 45 minutes.
Let the bonets cool in the refrigerator for least a couple of hours before you remove them from the molds.

Preparation time: 20’ Cooking time: 45’
Cooling time: 2 h Difficulty: easy

CHOCOLATE PUDDING

INGREDIENTS FOR 4 PEOPLE

4 egg yolks
generous 1/2 cup (110 g) sugar
generous 1 1/2 cups (400 ml) cream
1/4 cup (20 g) cocoa powder
3/4 oz (20 g) dark chocolate, chopped

METHOD

Put the cream in a saucepan and let it warm over low heat.
In a bowl, beat the egg yolks and sugar mixed with cocoa until frothy.
Slowly pour the hot cream onto the egg yolks and add the chopped chocolate, stirring well but avoiding foaming.
Pour the cream into suitable molds and bake in bain-marie at 210 °F (100 °C) for about an hour, until the pudding is firm.
Remove from the oven and leave to cool,
then let it rest in the refrigerator for at least 2 hours.

Preparation time: 15' Cooking time: 1 h
Cooling times: 2 h Difficulty: easy

SICILIAN CHOCOLATE CANNOLI

INGREDIENTS FOR 4 PEOPLE

For the dough
generous 1 1/2 cups (200 g) all-purpose flour
1/4 cup (20 g) cocoa powder
2 tbsp (25 g) sugar
2 eggs
3 tbsp (50 ml) Marsala
4 tsp (20 g) butter
salt
extra virgin olive oil for frying

For the filling
9 oz (250 g) fresh ricotta
1/2 cup (100 g) sugar
2 oz (50 g) candied orange peel
2 oz (50 g) chocolate, chopped

METHOD

On a pastry board, knead the flour, cocoa, butter, egg, sugar and a pinch of salt, and then add the Marsala.
Once you have a smooth dough, let it rest for about half an hour.
Meanwhile, prepare the filling.
Sieve the ricotta and mix it with sugar, then incorporate the candied orange peel and coarsely chopped chocolate. Put the filling in the refrigerator.
Roll out the dough and cut discs about 4 in (10 cm) in diameter, wrapping them around cannoli tubes. Fry the shells (with the tubes still in place) in plenty of hot oil for 1 to 2 minutes.
As soon as the shells of dough are golden brown, let them dry on paper towels and leave them to cool before removing them from the cannoli tubes.
Use a piping bag to stuff the cannoli with the ricotta filling and serve immediately.

Preparation time: 30' Resting time: 30'
Cooking time: 1-2' Difficulty: medium

FRIED CHOCOLATE CREMINI

INGREDIENTS FOR 4 PEOPLE

2 cups (500 ml) milk
1/4 cup (50 g) sugar
zest of half a lemon
scant 1 cup (120 g) semolina
2 egg yolks
1 egg
generous 3/4 cup (100 g) all-purpose flour
1/4 cup (20 g) cocoa powder
breadcrumbs
salt
extra virgin olive oil for frying
confectioners' (icing) sugar to finish

METHOD

In a saucepan, boil the milk and sugar mixed with cocoa, a pinch of salt, and the zest from half a lemon (make sure it has no pith).
Stir in the semolina and cook for a few minutes.
Remove from the heat and add the two egg yolks, making sure that they do not cook.
Roll out the dough on a greased baking sheet and leave to cool.
Cut the dough into small cubes or other shapes as desired.
Dip these chocolate cremini in flour, then in the beaten egg and finally in breadcrumbs.
Fry in hot oil, drain on absorbent paper, then sprinkle with a little sugar or icing sugar to taste.

Preparation time: 40' Cooking time: 10'
Difficulty: easy

MILK CHOCOLATE MOUSSE

INGREDIENTS FOR **6** PEOPLE

For the mousse
1 cup (250 ml) milk
2 egg yolks
9 oz (250 g) milk chocolate
7 oz (200 g) semi-whipped cream
1/3 oz (10 g) leaf gelatin

For the dough for the chocolate rolls
1/2 cup (100 g) sugar
3 eggs
1 egg yolk
2/3 cup (80 g) all-purpose flour
2 1/2 tbsp (20 g) potato starch
3 tbsp (15 g) cocoa powder

For the syrup
2 tbsp (30 ml) water
3/8 cup (80 g) sugar
2 1/2 tbsp (35 ml) rum
(or other liqueur of your choice)

METHOD

To make the dough for the chocolate rolls, sift together the flour, starch, and cocoa. Separate the eggs and whip the egg whites in a bowl with the sugar. Break the egg yolks into another bowl and stir with a fork. Fold in the egg whites, then add the flour sifted with cocoa and starch. Spread a layer of dough about a 3/8 in (1 cm) thick on a baking sheet lined with parchment paper. Bake at 450 °F (230° C) for 5 to 7 minutes.
Chop the chocolate and place in a bowl.
Soften the gelatin in cold water.
Dilute the egg yolks in the milk and pasteurize everything, bringing it to 185 °F (85 °C) on a low heat, stirring constantly.
Remove from heat and melt the squeezed gelatin.
Immediately pour it onto the chopped chocolate and stir thoroughly to obtain a smooth, even mixture. Let it cool to 86 °F (30° C).
In the meantime, whip the cream, which must stay fairly soft, then gently fold it in with a spatula.
Line the bottom and sides of a pastry ring with the dough and drench it with syrup (prepared by boiling water and sugar together, letting it cool, and then adding the rum). Fill with mousse. Smooth it out with a spatula and place in the refrigerator for at least 3 hours.
Remove from the mold and decorate as desired.

Preparation time: 45' + 25' (dough for the chocolate rolls) + 10' (syrup)
Cooling time: 3 h Difficulty: medium

WHITE CHOCOLATE MOUSSE WITH PEACH JELLY

INGREDIENTS FOR 4 PEOPLE

For the mousse
1/2 cup (125 ml) cream
9 oz (250 g) white chocolate
12 oz (325 g) semi-whipped cream

For the peach jelly
9 oz (250 g) yellow peach pulp
3/8 cup (75 g) sugar
1/3 oz (8 g) leaf gelatin

For the decoration
white chocolate chips

METHOD

Prepare the peach jelly. Soften the gelatin in cold water.
Puree the peach pulp, heating one-third of it in a saucepan with the sugar.
When it boils, add the squeezed gelatin, making sure it dissolves well.
Add the rest of the peach pulp and pour into individual cups or bowls.
Let it cool before adding the mousse.
For the mousse, chop the white chocolate and place in a bowl.
Boil the cream in a saucepan and pour over the chocolate,
stirring with a spatula until you have a smooth, soft cream.
Leave to cool to about 85 °F (30° C).
In the meantime, whip the cream. For the steps that follow,
it should remain fairly soft.
Fold the whipped cream into the cream and white chocolate mixture,
stirring gently with a spatula.
Pour the mousse over the peach jelly in the cups or bowls.
Leave in the refrigerator for at least 2 hours.
Garnish with shavings of white chocolate, made by scraping
a bar of chocolate against a knife held perpendicular to it.

Preparation time: 1 h + 30' Cooling time: 2 h
Difficulty: medium

DARK CHOCOLATE MOUSSE

INGREDIENTS FOR 4/6 PEOPLE

9 oz (250 g) dark chocolate
1 cup (250 ml) cream
5 oz (150 g) semi-whipped cream

METHOD

Chop the chocolate and place in a bowl.
Boil the cream in a saucepan and pour it over the chopped chocolate, then stir with a spatula until you have a smooth, soft cream.
Allow to cool to about 85 °F (30 °C).
In the meantime, whip the cream.
For the steps that follow, it should remain fairly soft.
Gently fold the semi-whipped cream into the chocolate mixture with a spatula.
Pour the resulting mousse into hemispherical silicone molds.
Freeze for at least 3 hours, until it has completely solidified.
Remove the mousse from the molds and allow to thaw.
Decorate it as desired: dark chocolate flakes are a good idea.

Preparation time: 30' Freezing time: 3 h
Difficulty: easy

ACADEMIA BARILLA
ACADEMIA BARILLA

CHOCOLATE PROFITEROLES

INGREDIENTS FOR 4 PEOPLE

7 oz (200 g) whipped cream

For the pastry cream (the minimum quantity for good results)
1 egg yolk
3 1/2 tbsp (40 g) sugar
4 tsp (10 g) all-purpose flour
1/2 cup (125 ml) milk
1/4 vanilla bean

For the profiteroles
6 3/4 (100 ml) water
3 1/2 tbsp (50 g) butter
1/2 cup (60 g) all-purpose flour
2 eggs
salt

For the covering sauce
3/8 cup (100 ml) cream
4 tsp (20 ml) glucose syrup (optional)
3 1/2 oz (100 g) dark chocolate

METHOD

For the puffs, put water, small pieces of butter, and a pinch of salt in a saucepan. Bring to the boil and empty the previously sifted flour into it all at once. Stir with a wooden spoon until everything is detached from the edges of the pan. Empty into a bowl, leave to cool, and stir in the eggs one at a time. Put the mixture into a piping bag with a 3/8 in (1 cm) nozzle and, on a lightly buttered, floured baking sheet, form cream puffs shaped like round door knobs. Bake at 400 °F (200 °C) for about 20 minutes, opening the oven door slightly during the last 5 minutes of cooking to allow them to dry.
For the pastry cream, heat the milk in a saucepan with a quarter of a vanilla bean cut open with a paring knife. Whisk the egg yolks and sugar together in a bowl, add the sifted flour and stir. Remove the vanilla bean from the milk. Pour a little hot milk on the eggs, add the remainder and let soften. Put in a saucepan and bring to the boil. Empty into a bowl and leave to cool. Combine the whipped cream with 1/2 cup (120 ml) pastry cream. The moment they cool down, fill the cream puffs with a piping bag, using a 1/10 in (2 mm) nozzle through holes at the bottom. Store in the refrigerator until ready to serve.
For a covering sauce, chop the chocolate and put in a bowl. In a small saucepan, boil the cream with the glucose syrup and pour it over the chocolate. Stir with a spatula to obtain a velvety, smooth cream. Skewer the cream puffs with a fork and cover with the chocolate sauce. Drain and place each one on the serving plate.

Preparation time: 1 h + 25' (pastry cream)
Difficulty: hard

CHOCOLATE PUDDING

INGREDIENTS FOR 4 PEOPLE

For the cream

2 cups (500 ml) milk
3 eggs
3/4 cup (150 g) sugar
3/8 cup (30 g) cocoa powder
3 oz (80 g) dark chocolate
butter for greasing the molds

For the chocolate sponge cake (the minimum quantity for good results)

3 eggs
generous 3/8 cup (80 g) sugar
generous 3/8 cup (50 g) all-purpose flour
2 tbsp (10 g) cocoa powder
2 tbsp (15 g) potato starch
2 tsp (10 g) butter
1/2 tsp (2 g) baking powder (optional)
vanilla powder

METHOD

Prepare the chocolate sponge cake. In a bain-marie, lightly heat the eggs with the sugar, stirring with a whisk. Beat the mixture (preferably with a mixer) and then carefully incorporate the flour, cocoa, starch, a pinch of vanilla powder, and the baking powder (sifted together), stirring from bottom to top with a spatula. Finally, add the warm, melted butter.
Fill a buttered, floured cake tin two-thirds full.
Bake in the oven at 340 °F (170 °C) for 20 to 25 minutes.
Prepare the cream, beating the eggs and sugar mixed with cocoa in a bowl.
Boil the milk and pour a quarter on the compound to 'temper' it, mixing well.
Then, add the remaining milk. Stir in the chopped chocolate.
Cut 3 1/2 oz (100 g) of sponge cake into cubes and place in four individual, previously buttered, molds. Pour in the cream and bake in a bain-marie at 300 °F (150 °C) for 50 minutes.
Let the chocolate pudding cool for about 2 hours at room temperature, then remove from the molds.

Preparation time: 20' + 55' (chocolate sponge cake)
Cooking time: 50' Resting time: 2 h Difficulty: easy

CHOCOLATE ZUCCOTTO

INGREDIENTS FOR 4 PEOPLE

For the chocolate sponge cake (the minimum quantity for good results)
3 eggs
generous 3/8 cup (80 g) sugar
generous 3/8 cup (50 g) all-purpose flour
2 tbsp (10 g) cocoa powder
2 tbsp (15 g) potato starch
2 tsp (10 g) butter
1/2 tsp (2 g) baking powder (optional)
vanilla powder

For the Italian meringue
2 oz (60 g) egg whites
5/8 cup (120 g) sugar
4 tsp (20 g) water

For the cream
9 oz (250 g) ricotta
1 1/4 oz (35 g) chocolate
3 tbsp (15 g) cocoa

For the syrup
2 tbsp (30 ml) water
generous 3/8 cup (80 g) sugar
2 1/2 tbsp (35 ml) orange liqueur

For the decoration
13 1/2 oz (100 g) dark chocolate
scant 1/2 cup (50 g) chopped toasted hazelnuts

METHOD

For the sponge cake (for this recipe you will need 11 oz/250 grams), gently heat the eggs and sugar in a bain-marie, stirring with a whisk. Beat and then incorporate the flour, cocoa, starch, a pinch of vanilla powder, and baking powder (all sifted together), stirring from the bottom to the top with a spatula. Finally, add the warm, melted butter. Fill a buttered, floured cake tin two-thirds full. Bake at 340 °F (170 °C) for 20–25 minutes.
For the meringue, heat 1/2 cup (105 g) sugar with 4 tsp (20 ml) water, bringing it to 250 °F (121 °C). Beat 2 oz (60 g) egg whites with 5 tsp (15 g) sugar. When the egg mixture has stiffened, the sugar will have cooked: keep beating the eggs, however, until everything is lukewarm.
Pass the ricotta through a sieve, divide it into two bowls.
Add sifted cocoa to one and the chopped chocolate to the other.
Stir 3 oz (75 g) of meringue mixture into each one.
Cut the sponge cake into slices and place them inside a spherical mold, previously lined with plastic wrap for easy unmolding.
Sprinkle with orange syrup, prepared by boiling sugar and water, letting it cool and then adding the orange liqueur.
Cover the mold with then chocolate cream, then fill with the white one with chopped chocolate.
Close with more slices of soaked sponge cake and freeze for at least 2 to 3 hours.
Remove from the freezer 10 minutes before serving. Cover with warm, melted chocolate, and sprinkle with chopped hazelnuts.

Preparation time: 1 h + 55' (sponge) + 10' (syrup)
Freezing time: 2-3 h Difficulty: hard

ZUPPA INGLESE

INGREDIENTS FOR 4 PEOPLE

For the chocolate sponge cake (the minimum quantity for good results)
3 eggs
generous 3/8 cup (80 g) sugar
generous 3/8 cup (50 g) all-purpose flour
2 tbsp (10 g) cocoa
2 tbsp (15 g) potato starch
2 tsp (10 g) butter
1/2 tsp (2 g) baking powder (optional)
vanilla powder

For the pastry cream
3 egg yolks
generous 1/2 cup (115 g) sugar
1/4 cup (30 g) all-purpose flour
1 1/2 cups (375 ml) milk
1/2 a vanilla bean
1/8 cup (12 g) cocoa
1 oz (30 g) dark chocolate, chopped

For the syrup
2 tbsp (30 ml) water
generous 3/8 cup (80 g) sugar
2 1/2 tbsp (35 ml) Alkermes liqueur

For the decoration
7 oz (200 g) sweetened whipped cream

METHOD

For the sponge cake (for this recipe you will need 200 g/7 oz), gently heat the eggs and sugar in a bain-marie, stirring with a whisk. Beat and then incorporate the flour, cocoa, starch, a pinch of vanilla powder, and baking powder (all sifted together), stirring from the bottom to the top with a spatula. Finally, add the warm, melted butter. Fill two-thirds of a buttered, floured cake tin. Bake at 340 °F (170 °C) for 20 to 25 minutes.

For the pastry cream, heat the milk in a saucepan with half a vanilla bean (cut open lengthways with a paring knife). Beat the egg yolks in a bowl with sugar, add the sifted flour, and stir. Remove the vanilla bean from the milk. Pour a little boiling milk on the eggs, then gradually add the rest of the milk to temper them, whisking all the time. Put in the saucepan and bring to the boil. Divide the cream equally between two containers. Flavor one bowl by dissolving the cocoa powder and finely chopped dark chocolate into it while the cream is still hot. Leave to cool.

Cut the sponge cake to a thickness of 3/8 in (1 cm) and the diameter of the containers used.

Place a piece of sponge at the bottom of each mold and drench it with the Alkermes syrup, prepared by boiling sugar and water together, letting it cool, and then adding the liqueur.

With a piping bag, add a layer of vanilla cream, then superimpose another piece of sponge cake and drench it in turn. Add a layer of the chocolate cream; then cover with a final layer of sponge cake and drench it again. Refrigerate for an hour. Serve garnished with sweetened whipped cream.

Preparation time: 30' + 30' (vanilla and chocolate pastry cream) + 55' (sponge) + 10' (syrup)
Cooling time: 1 h Difficulty: easy

Gourmet Snacks

CHOCOLATE CEREAL BARS

INGREDIENTS FOR 4 PEOPLE

7 oz (200 g) dark chocolate
3 1/2 oz (100 g) corn flakes
1 3/4 oz (50 g) rice crispies
generous 1/8 cup (20 g) pistachios (shelled)
3/4 oz (20 g) candied orange peel

METHOD

Cut the candied orange peel into cubes, mix it with the corn flakes and rice crispies, then add the pistachios.
To prepare the tempered dark chocolate: melt the chocolate in a bain-marie or microwave at 115-120 °F (45-50° C) (use a cooking thermometer), then pour one-third to one-half onto a marble surface. Let this cool until it reaches 80 °F (26-27 °C), then add it on top of the remaining hot chocolate.
When the temperature of this new mixture reaches 90 °F (31-32° C), it is ready to be used.
Add the tempered chocolate into the mixture and mix well.
Pour the mixture onto a baking sheet lined with parchment paper, smoothing it out with a spatula to a thickness of 3/4-1 1/4 in (2-3 cm).
Leave to cool and harden in the refrigerator for 5 minutes, then, with a knife, cut the chocolate cereal bars into the required shapes and sizes.

Preparation time: 15' Cooling time: 5'
Difficulty: easy

GIANDUIA CREAM SPREAD

INGREDIENTS FOR ONE JAR

4 1/2 oz (125 g) dark chocolate
4 1/2 oz (125 g) milk chocolate
1/3 cup (100 g) hazelnut paste
3 tbsp (50 ml) light extra virgin olive oil

METHOD

In a bain-marie or microwave, melt both the dark chocolate and milk chocolate in separate containers. Combine the two types of chocolate with the hazelnut paste and then add the extra virgin olive oil (choose a light, delicate variety).
Stir well until it is warmed through but do not let it begin to thicken.
Pour the gianduia cream into a glass jar.
This spread does not need to be refrigerated. Store in a cool, dry place.

Preparation time: 25'
Difficulty: easy

PUFFED RICE AND CHOCOLATE LOLLIPOPS

INGREDIENTS FOR 4 PEOPLE

For the lollipops
4 puffed rice cakes

For the glaze
5 oz (150 g) dark chocolate

For the decoration
1/3 cup (40 g) dried nuts to taste
(chopped toasted hazelnuts,
toasted almonds, unsalted pistachio nuts...)

METHOD

Stick a wooden skewer through each of the rice cakes.
To prepare the tempered dark chocolate: melt the chocolate in a bain-marie or microwave at 113–122 °F (45–50° C) (use a cooking thermometer), then pour one-third to one-half onto a marble surface. Let this cool until it reaches 79–81 °F (26–27 °C), then add it on top of the remaining hot chocolate. When the temperature of this new mixture reaches 88–90 °F (31–32° C), it is ready to be used.
Dip the lollipops in the tempered chocolate, drain the excess, and place them on a plate lined with parchment paper. Sprinkle immediately with nuts (this can include chopped toasted hazelnuts, toasted almonds, unsalted pistachio nuts, and more...).
Let the lollipops crystallize at room temperature.

Preparation time: 10'
Difficulty: easy

CARAMEL TOFFEE AND MILK CHOCOLATE SNACKS

INGREDIENTS FOR 8 BARS

For the shortbread pastry
1 1/4 cups (165 g) all-purpose flour
scant 1/2 cup (100 g) butter
generous 3/8 cup (85 g) sugar
1 egg
1/4 tsp (1 g) baking powder (optional)
vanilla powder
salt

For the caramel toffee
1/2 cup (100 g) sugar
3 tbsp (50 ml) cream
4 tsp (20 ml) water

For the glaze
7 oz (200 g) milk chocolate

For the decoration
1 1/2 oz (40 g) toasted almond sticks

METHOD

Prepare the shortbread pastry. Mix the softened butter with the sugar, then stir in a pinch of salt and the egg. Add flour sifted with baking powder and a pinch of vanilla powder. Knead briefly until you have a smooth, even dough. Wrap the dough in plastic wrap and leave to rest in the refrigerator for one hour.

On a floured surface, roll out the dough with a rolling pin to a thickness of 1/8 in (3 mm). Cut rectangles of 1 1/2 x 3 1/2 in (4 x 9 cm) and arrange them on a baking sheet lined with parchment paper.

Bake at 350 °F (180 °C) for 12 minutes. Leave to cool.

Prepare the caramel toffee. Put the sugar in a wide saucepan and add water. Cook on high heat until it turns a dark, golden color. Heat the cream in another pan, then stir it into the sugar and let it boil until a thick sauce has formed. Leave to cool.

Spread a little toffee on half the shortbread bars, then superimpose another on each one. Leave to cool.

To temper the milk chocolate: melt the chocolate in a bain-marie or microwave at 113–122 °F (45–50° C) (use a cooking thermometer), then pour one-third to one-half onto a marble surface. Let this cool until it reaches 79–81 °F (26–27 °C), then add it on top of the remaining hot chocolate. When the temperature of this new mixture reaches 86–88 °F (30–31°C), it is ready to be used.

For the icing, dip the fingers in the tempered milk chocolate, then place them on a sheet of parchment paper and sprinkle with almonds. Once the chocolate has crystallized, repeat the icing process.

Preparation time: 1 h + 20' (shortbread pastry)
Resting time: 1 h Difficulty: high

CHOCOLATE SLICES

INGREDIENTS FOR 4 PEOPLE

For the dough (chocolate rolls)
1/2 cup (100 g) sugar
3 eggs
1 egg yolk
2/3 cup (80 g) all-purpose flour
2 1/2 tbsp (20 g) potato starch
3 tbsp (15 g) cocoa powder

For the chocolate ice cream base
2 cups (500 ml) milk
5/8 cup (130 g) sugar
scant 5/8 cup (50 g) cocoa powder
1/2 oz (15 g) dextrose
1/8 oz (3.5 g) stabilizer
1/3 oz (10 g) dark chocolate
4 tbsp (50 g) hazelnut paste
1 tbsp (20 g) honey

For the glaze
3 1/2 oz (100 g) dark chocolate

METHOD

For the chocolate roll dough, sift together flour, starch, and cocoa. Separate the eggs and whip the egg whites and sugar in a bowl. Break up the egg yolks with a fork in a separate bowl and fold in the egg whites. Then add the sifted flour and cocoa with the starch. Spread a layer of dough about 3/8 in (1 cm) thick on a baking sheet lined with parchment paper. Bake at 450 °F (230° C) for 5 to 7 minutes.
Prepare the base for the chocolate ice cream (see recipe). After leaving it to 'ripen' at 4°C for 6 hours, add 500 grams to the hazelnut paste and the honey, then mix it all together with a hand blender.
Freeze the mixture in an ice cream maker until you have an ice cream that is fluffy and dry-looking, and not shiny (how long this takes depends on what kind of ice cream maker you use).
Cut the layer of dough for the rolls in half and spread the ice cream on one of the pieces. Superimpose the second half and level it. Put it in the freezer for 30 minutes to harden, then cut into squares or triangles.
Meanwhile, to temper the chocolate: melt the chocolate in a bain-marie or microwave at 113–122 °F (45–50° C) (use a cooking thermometer), then pour one-third to one-half onto a marble surface. Let this cool until it reaches 79–81 °F (26–27 °C), then add it on top of the remaining hot chocolate. When the temperature of this new mixture reaches 86–88 °F (30–31°C), it is ready to be used.
Ice one side of the slices with the tempered chocolate.

Preparation time: 1 h + 25' (dough for the chocolate rolls) + 20' (ice cream)
Ice cream ripening time: 6 h Freezing time: 30' Difficulty: medium

Sophisticated Pralines

CHOCOLATE KISSES

INGREDIENTS FOR 4 PEOPLE

For the chocolate shortbread pastry*
1 1/4 cups (165 g) all-purpose flour
3/8 cup (95 g) butter
scant 1/2 cup (85 g) sugar
2 egg yolks
1/4 tsp (1 g) baking powder (optional)
7 tsp (9 g) cocoa powder
vanilla powder
salt

For the chocolate sponge cake*
3 eggs
scant 1/2 cup (85 g) sugar
generous 3/8 cup (50 g) all-purpose flour
2 tbsp (10 g) cocoa
2 tbsp (15 g) potato starch
2 tsp (10 g) butter
1/2 tsp (2 g) baking powder (optional)
vanilla powder
6 1/2 oz (187 g) cookies
1/4 cup (25 g) cocoa
2 1/2 tbsp (35 ml) rum

For the syrup
3 tbsp (40 ml) water
3/8 cup (80 g) sugar

For the glaze
65 oz (150 g) dark chocolate

For the decoration
1/4 cup (30 g) hazelnuts and pistachios

***the minimum quantity for good results**

METHOD

Prepare the syrup by boiling the sugar and water together for two minutes. Leave it to cool. For the sponge cake, lightly heat the eggs and sugar in a bain-marie, stirring with a whisk. Beat and then incorporate the flour, cocoa, starch, a pinch of vanilla powder, and baking powder (all sifted together), stirring from the bottom to the top with a spatula. Finally, add the warm, melted butter. Fill two-thirds of a buttered, floured cake tin. Bake at 340 °F (170 °C) for 20 to 25 minutes.
For the shortbread pastry, mix the softened butter with the sugar, then stir in a pinch of salt and the egg. Add the flour sifted with baking powder, cocoa and a pinch of vanilla powder. Knead briefly until you have a smooth, even dough. Wrap the dough in plastic wrap and leave to rest in the refrigerator for one hour. On a floured work surface, roll out 3 1/2 oz (100 g) of the dough with a rolling pin to a thickness of 1/10 in (2 mm). Cut discs 1 1/4 in (3 cm) in diameter with a pastry ring and arrange on a baking sheet lined with parchment paper. Bake at 350 °F (180 °C) for 8 to 9 minutes. Remove from the oven and leave to cool. Put the crumbled cookies in the food processor with 6 1/2 oz (187 g) diced chocolate sponge cake, cocoa, and rum, then drench with 1/4-1/3 cup (70-90 ml) of syrup to obtain an even paste, smooth but not too soft. Using a piping bag with a nozzle of 5/8 in (1.5 cm), form cones with this paste on the dough disks. Leave in the refrigerator for 15 minutes to solidify.
To temper the chocolate: melt the chocolate in a bain-marie or a microwave until it reaches 113-122 °F (45-50° C) (use a cooking thermometer), then pour one-third to half on a marble surface. Let it cool until it drops to 79-81 °F (26-27 °C), then add this on top of the still-warm remainder. When this reaches 88-90 °F (31-32° C), it is ready to be used. Glaze the cones by dipping them in the tempered chocolate. Before the chocolate hardens, decorate with chopped hazelnuts and pistachios.

Preparation time: 1 h + 20' (shortbread pastry) + 55' (sponge) + 10' (syrup) Resting time: 1 h Difficulty: medium

HEMINGWAY'S CHOCOLATES (CUNEESI AL RUM)

INGREDIENTS FOR 25 CUNEESI

For the meringue
1 egg white
1/3 cup (60 g) sugar
2 tsp (3 g) cocoa powder

For the filling
1/4 cup (50 ml) cream
scant 1/4 cup (50 ml) glucose syrup
5 oz (150 g) dark chocolate
2 tsp (10 g) hazelnut paste
1/2 cup (125 ml) rum
vanilla powder

For the pastry cream (the minimum quantity for good results)
1 egg yolk
3 1/2 tbsp (40 g) sugar
4 tsp (10 g) all-purpose flour
1/2 cup (125 ml) milk
1/4 vanilla bean

For the glaze
5 oz (150 g) dark chocolate

METHOD

Whip the egg white in a bowl with a whisk. When halfway done, add one-third of the sugar and continue to whip until they have stiffened but are not spongy. Fold in the remaining sugar, mixed with the cocoa, stirring from the top to the bottom with a spatula. On a baking sheet lined with parchment paper, shape into meringues the size of a walnut using a piping bag with a 3/8 in (1 cm) nozzle. Bake at 375 °F (190°C) for about 20 minutes. Just as they are finished cooking, gently remove from the paper and, with your thumb, lightly press in the bottom, creating a slight hollow.
For the pastry cream, heat the milk in a saucepan with a quarter of a vanilla bean, cut open lengthways with a paring knife. Cream the yolk and sugar in a bowl, add the sifted flour and stir. Remove the vanilla bean from the milk. Pour a little boiling milk on the eggs, then gradually add the rest of the milk to temper them, whisking all the time. Put in a saucepan and bring to the boil. Pour into a bowl and leave to cool.
To prepare the filling: chop the chocolate and put it in a bowl, then boil the cream with the glucose syrup and pour it over the chocolate. Mix well until you have a smooth, silky cream.
Add the hazelnut paste, a pinch of vanilla, and rum.
Mix together and, finally, add a scant 1/4 cup (50 ml) of the pastry cream.
Let harden, then stick meringues together in pairs with the filling.
To temper the chocolate: melt it in a bain-marie or a microwave until it reaches 113–122 °F (45–50° C) (use a cooking thermometer), then pour one-third to half on a marble surface. Let it cool until it drops to 79–81 °F (26–27 °C), then add this on top of the still-warm remainder.
When this reaches 86–88 °F (30–31°C), it is ready to be used.
Glaze the cuneesi with the tempered chocolate.

Preparation time: 3 h + 25' (pastry cream)
Difficulty: high

CHOCOLATE-COVERED ALMONDS AND HAZELNUTS

INGREDIENTS FOR 4 PEOPLE

1 1/2 tbsp (20 g) sugar
2 tsp (10 ml) water
1 cup (125 g) almonds and hazelnuts
1 tsp (5 g) butter
6 oz (180 g) dark chocolate

METHOD

Put the sugar and water in a saucepan and bring to a boil. Add the almonds and hazelnuts, then cook until the sugar is amber in color. Stir in the butter, then pour the mixture onto a baking sheet so that it cools, separating the almonds and hazelnuts.
Once it has cooled down, put it in a large bowl and add about a quarter of the chocolate, previously melted in a bain-marie or microwave. Stir so that the chocolate does not solidify, keeping the almonds and hazelnuts well separated.
Repeat until you have finished all of the chocolate.
Place the chocolate-coated nuts in a sieve with a large mesh so that the excess chocolate drains off, then store in a dry place at room temperature, preferably in sealed glass jars or in cans with a lid.

Preparation time: 40'
Difficulty: easy

MARASCHINO PARMIGIANI

INGREDIENTS FOR ABOUT **25** PARMIGIANI

For the cookies
1 cup (125 g) roasted hazelnuts
1/4 egg white
1 1/4 cups (250 g) sugar
scant 5/8 cup (50 g) cocoa powder
vanilla powder

For the filling
2 tbsp (30 ml) water
1/3 cup (60 g) sugar
1/3 cup (75 ml) Maraschino
9 oz (250 g) dark chocolate

For the glaze
6 oz (150 g) milk chocolate

METHOD

Finely grind the hazelnuts and sugar in a blender, using the pulse feature. Put a pinch of vanilla powder and cocoa in a bowl, then mix with the egg white needed to make an even paste, smooth but not too soft). On a buttered, floured baking sheet, form walnut-sized disks of dough using a piping bag with a 3/4 in (2 cm) nozzle. Bake at 350 °F (180 °C) for about 18 minutes. Remove from the oven and, before they are completely cool, remove the cookies from the sheet. Boil the water and sugar to obtain a syrup, then cover and leave to cool. Take 1/3 cup (75 ml) of the syrup, add the liqueur to it, and then the dark chocolate, previously melted in a bain-marie or a microwave. Let the filling thicken and, when it has a creamy consistency, add it to the cookies. To temper the milk chocolate: melt the chocolate in a bain-marie or a microwave until it reaches 113–122 °F (45–50° C) (use a cooking thermometer), then pour one-third to half on a marble surface. Let it cool until it drops to 79–81 °F (26–27 °C), then add this on top of the still-warm remainder. When this reaches 86–88 °F (30–31°C), it is ready to be used. Glaze the parmigiani, dipping them in the tempered milk chocolate.

Preparation time: 3 h
Cooking time: 18' Difficulty: high

CHOCOLATE SALAMI

INGREDIENTS FOR ONE SALAMI

2 oz (50 g) dry biscuits
5 tsp (25 g) butter
4 oz (120 g) hazelnut chocolate
1 tbsp (10 g) roasted hazelnuts
1 tbsp (10 g) pistachios
1 tbsp (10 g) pine nuts
1 tbsp (10 g) sweet almonds
confectioners' (powdered) sugar

METHOD

Coarsely crumble the biscuits in a bowl, then add the toasted hazelnuts, pistachios, pine nuts, and sweet almonds, and mix.
Melt the hazelnut chocolate, let it cool and then pour it over everything, also adding the softened butter.
Let the mixture harden just enough so that you can still manipulate it.
Mix well and form a sausage shape on a work surface covered with confectioners' (icing) sugar.
Sprinkle more confectioners' sugar over it and then wrap in waxed paper, tying it with a kitchen string to look like a real salami.

Preparation time: 3 h
Difficulty: easy

CHOCOLATE-COVERED ORANGE PEELS

INGREDIENTS FOR 4 PEOPLE

For the peels
4 1/2 oz (130 g) candied orange peel in quarters

For the glaze
2 1/2 oz (70 g) dark chocolate

METHOD

Arrange the candied orange peel quarters on a wire rack and leave to dry at room temperature overnight.
The next day, cut the orange peels into strips about 1/4 in (5-6 mm) wide and temper the dark chocolate: melt the chocolate in a bain-marie or microwave at 113–122 °F (45–50° C) (use a cooking thermometer), then pour one-third to one-half onto a marble surface. Let this cool until it reaches 79–81 °F (26–27 °C), then add it on top of the remaining hot chocolate. When the temperature of this new mixture reaches 86–88 °F (30–31°C), it is ready to be used.
Glaze the candied orange peels in tempered chocolate using a fork.
Drain the excess chocolate and place the frosted sticks on a sheet of parchment paper.
Let the chocolate-covered orange peels crystallize at room temperature.

Preparation time: 12 h
Difficulty: easy

ASSORTED TRUFFLES

INGREDIENTS FOR 12 PEOPLE

For the black truffles

2 1/4 oz (65 g) dark chocolate
3/8 cup (50 g) toasted hazelnuts, chopped
1 cup (100 g) confectioners' (powdered) sugar
1/8 cup (12 g) cocoa powder
4 tsp (20 ml) light extra virgin olive oil
sweetened or unsweetened cocoa

For the white truffles

2 oz (60 g) white chocolate
4 1/2 tbsp (60 g) hazelnut paste
3 tbsp (25 g) toasted hazelnuts, chopped
5/8 cup (65 g) confectioners' (powdered) sugar
2 tsp (2 g) cocoa powder
confectioners' (powdered) sugar to finish

For the pistachio truffles

3 1/2 oz (100 g) white chocolate
3 1/2 tbsp (30 g) pistachios, chopped
4 tsp (25 g) pistachio paste
3 1/2 oz (100 g) white chocolate for finishing
confectioners' (powdered) sugar for the work surface
generous 3/8 cup (50 g) chopped pistachios for finishing

METHOD

For the black truffles, melt the chocolate and stir together well with the other ingredients, adding a little of the oil from time to time as needed.
On a work surface dusted with cocoa, roll into lengths, then cut into chunks. Form the pieces into truffle shapes (they need not be uniform) and roll them in the cocoa.
For white truffles, melt the white chocolate and stir together well with the other ingredients.
On a work surface dusted with confectioners' sugar, roll into lengths, then cut into chunks.
Form the pieces into truffle shapes and dip them in sugar.
For the pistachio truffles, melt the white chocolate and stir together well with the other ingredients.
On a work surface dusted with confectioners' sugar, roll into lengths, then cut into chunks. Roll them into a ball and 'dirty' them with a thin layer of warm, melted white chocolate. Immediately roll the truffles in the chopped pistachios, ensuring that they adhere well.

Preparation time: 45'
Difficulty: easy

Slices of Sweetness

WHITE CHOCOLATE AND RASPBERRY TART

INGREDIENTS FOR 4 PEOPLE

For the chocolate shortbread pastry (the minimum quantity for good results)

1 1/4 cups (165 g) all-purpose flour
3/8 cup (95 g) butter
generous 3/8 cup (85 g) sugar
2 egg yolks
1/4 tsp (1 g) baking powder (optional)
7 tsp (9 g) cocoa powder
vanilla powder
salt

For the filling

generous 3/8 cup (100 ml) cream
2 tsp (10 ml) glucose syrup
7 oz (200 g) white chocolate
3 oz (80 g) raspberry jam

For the decoration

9 oz (250 g) fresh raspberries
confectioners' (icing) sugar

METHOD

Prepare the shortbread pastry. Mix the softened butter with the sugar, stir in a pinch of salt and the egg. Add the flour sifted with baking powder, cocoa and a pinch of vanilla powder, then knead briefly until you have a smooth, even paste. Wrap the dough in plastic wrap and leave to rest in the refrigerator for one hour.
On a floured surface, use a rolling pin to roll out 9 oz (250 g) of the shortbread pastry to a thickness of 1/8 in (3 mm).
Line a buttered, floured cake tin with the pastry.
Spread with raspberry jam and bake at 350 °F (180 °C) for 18 to 20 minutes.
Remove from the oven and leave to cool, then remove the tart from the tin.
Chop the white chocolate and put it in a bowl. Boil the cream with the glucose syrup in a saucepan and pour it over the chocolate.
Mix well until you have smooth, velvety cream.
Leave to cool and pour into the tart shell until it is filled up to the brim.
Garnish with fresh raspberries, which have been washed and dried, and put the cake to cool in the refrigerator for at least an hour.
Sprinkle with confectioners' sugar before serving.

Preparation time: 45' + 20' (shortbread pastry) Resting time: 1 h
Cooking time: 18-20' Cooling time: 1 h Difficulty: medium

CHOCOLATE RICOTTA TART

INGREDIENTS FOR 4 PEOPLE

For the shortbread pastry (the minimum quantity for good results)
1 1/4 cups (165 g) all-purpose flour
scant 1/2 cup (100 g) butter
generous 3/8 cup (85 g) sugar
1 egg
1/4 tsp (1 g) baking powder (optional)
vanilla powder
salt

For the filling
5 oz (150 g) ricotta
2 tbsp (30 g) butter
3 tbsp (35 g) sugar
4 tsp (10 g) all-purpose flour
salt
vanilla powder

For the ganache
3/8 cup (100 ml) cream
2 tsp (10 ml) glucose syrup
3 1/2 oz (100 g) dark chocolate

METHOD

Prepare the shortbread pastry. Mix the softened butter with the sugar, then stir in a pinch of salt and the egg. Add the flour sifted with baking powder and a pinch of vanilla powder. Knead briefly until you have a smooth, even dough. Wrap the dough in plastic wrap and leave to rest in the refrigerator for one hour.
On a floured surface, use a rolling pin to roll out 9 oz (250 g) of shortbread pastry to a thickness of 3 mm.
Line a buttered, floured cake tin with the pastry.
Pass the ricotta through a sieve, then knead in a bowl with sugar, salt, and vanilla powder. Add the sifted flour, then the warm, melted butter.
Work everything together well, then place on the bottom of the pie tin and bake at 340 °F (170 °C) for 25 to 30 minutes.
Remove from the oven and leave to cool, then remove the tart from the tin.
Prepare the ganache. Chop the chocolate and place in a bowl. Boil the cream in a saucepan with the glucose syrup and pour in the chocolate.
Mix well until you have a smooth, velvety cream.
Leave to cool and pour into the tart until it is full to the brim
Leave to cool in the refrigerator for at least an hour. Decorate as desired.

Preparation time: 45' + 20' (shortbread pastry)
Resting time: 1 h Cooking time: 25-30' Difficulty: medium

CHOCOLATE CAKE WITH WHIPPED CREAM AND CHERRIES

INGREDIENTS FOR 6 PEOPLE

For the chocolate sponge cake
3 eggs
generous 3/8 cup (80 g) sugar
generous 3/8 cup (50 g) all-purpose flour
2 tbsp (10 g) cocoa powder
2 tbsp (15 g) cornstarch (cornflour)
2 tsp (10 g) butter
1/2 tsp (2 g) baking powder (optional)
vanilla powder

For the filling
10 oz (300 g) sweetened whipped cream
9 oz (250 g) of pitted cherries
1/4 cup (30 g) cornstarch
juice of half a lemon
3/4 cup (150 g) sugar

For the syrup (the minimum quantity for good results)
2 tbsp (30 ml) water
generous 3/8 cup (80 g) sugar
2 1/2 tbsp (35 ml) Maraschino

For the decoration
milk chocolate chips
confectioners' (icing) sugar

METHOD

For the sponge cake, heat the eggs and sugar gently in a bain-marie, stirring with a whisk. Beat (preferably with a mixer) and then incorporate the flour, cocoa, starch, a pinch of vanilla powder, and baking powder, stirring from the bottom to the top with a spatula. Finally, add the warm, melted butter. Fill two-thirds of a greased and floured mold (a rectangular shape is recommended). Bake in the oven at 340 °F (170 °C) for 20 to 25 minutes. Remove from the mold and leave to cool (if possible, prepare this the day before and store in a paper bag: it will then be easier to cut without breaking it).
For the filling, mix the cornstarch with the sugar and combine it with the cherries in a saucepan. Bring to the boil. Boil for 1 to 2 minutes and add the juice of half a lemon. Let it cool completely.
For the maraschino syrup, boil sugar and water together, let it cool, then add the liqueur. For this recipe, you will need about 3/8 cup (100 ml) of syrup.
Cut the cake into two layers. Drench the bottom layer with the syrup and cover with the cherry compote. Spread with a layer whipped cream, sweetened to taste. Put the second layer of sponge cake on top. Drench with the syrup, then completely cover the surface and edges of the cake by spreading the remaining whipped cream over it. Garnish with chocolate shavings (made by scraping a chocolate bar with a knife held perpendicular to the chocolate bar), and refrigerate for at least an hour.
Sprinkle with confectioners' sugar before serving.

Preparation time: 50' + 55' (sponge) + 10' (syrup)
Cooling time: 1 h Difficulty: medium

CHOCOLATE RED WINE CAKE

INGREDIENTS FOR 4 PEOPLE

For the cake
3 1/2 tbsp (50 g) butter
1 oz (30 g) of melted chocolate
1/3 cup (30 g) confectioners' (icing) sugar
1 egg yolk
1 egg white
2 1/2 tbsp (30 g) sugar
scant 5/8 cup (75 g) all-purpose flour
1/4 cup (30 g) crushed walnuts
3 1/2 tbsp (50 ml) red wine
vanilla powder
cinnamon powder

For the ganache
3/8 cup (100 ml) cream
2 tsp (10 ml) glucose syrup
3 1/2 oz (100 g) dark chocolate

METHOD

Grind the walnuts in a food processor and mix in the sifted flour with a pinch of vanilla and cinnamon.
In a bowl, cream together the butter (softened at room temperature) and the confectioners' (powdered) sugar with a whisk. Add the warm, melted chocolate.
Add the yolk, then incorporate the flour and the nuts.
Add the wine and mix well.
Beat the egg white with a whisk. When halfway done, add the sugar and continue until the cream is stiff.
Using a spatula, gently fold the whipped egg white into the dough, stirring from the top to the bottom.
Grease and flour a plum cake mold and fill it three-quarters full with the mixture.
Bake at 340 °F (170 °C) for about an hour, remove from the mold and leave to cool completely.
Prepare the ganache. Chop the chocolate and place in a bowl. Boil the cream and the glucose syrup in a saucepan and pour on the chocolate. Mix well with a soft spatula (do not use a whisk since it would incorporates too much air, which will lead to bubbles) until you have a smooth and velvety cream.
Use this to frost the cake. Decorate the cake as desired.

Preparation time: 45'
Cooking time: 1 h Difficulty: medium

CHOCOLATE ALMOND TORTE (TORTA CAPRESE)

INGREDIENTS FOR 4 PEOPLE

scant 1/3 cup (70 g) butter
5/8 cup (60 g) confectioners' (icing) sugar
1 egg
1 egg yolk
2 1/2 oz (75 g) dark chocolate
1/3 cup (50 g) blanched almonds
confectioners' (powdered) sugar for finishing

METHOD

Mix the almonds with a quarter of the sugar and grind in a food processor.
Melt the chocolate in a bowl in a bain-marie or microwave.
In another bowl, cream the butter, softened at room temperature, and the remaining sugar together well.
Separate the egg, add the two yolks and continue beating.
Add the warm, melted chocolate, then incorporate the ground almonds.
Whip the egg white and fold very gently into the mixture, using a spatula and mixing from the bottom up.
Take any kind of cake tin, buttered and floured, or lined with parchment paper. Fill it three-quarters full, then bake in the oven at 325 °F (160 °C) for 40 to 45 minutes.
Leave to cool, remove from the tin, dust with confectioners' (icing) sugar, and decorate as desired.

Preparation time: 30'
Cooking time: 45' Difficulty: easy

CAKE WITH PEACHES, ALMONDS AND COCOA

INGREDIENTS FOR 6 PEOPLE

For the chocolate shortbread pastry*
1 1/4 cups (165 g) all-purpose flour
3/8 cup (95 g) butter
generous 3/8 cup (85 g) sugar
2 egg yolks
1/4 tsp (1 g) baking powder (optional)
7 tsp (9 g) cocoa powder
vanilla powder
salt
* **the minimum quantity for good results**

For the chocolate pastry cream*
1 egg yolk
3 1/2 tbsp (40 g) sugar
4 tsp (10 g) all-purpose flour
1/2 cup (125 ml) milk
1/4 vanilla bean
6 tsp (8 g) cocoa
2/3 oz (20 g) dark chocolate

For the filling
3 fresh or canned peaches
3 eggs
3 egg yolks
generous 1/2 cup (110 g) sugar
scant 5/8 cup (75 g) all-purpose flour
2 1/2 tbsp (20 g) potato starch
5/8 cup (80 g) almonds
2 tbsp (10 g) cocoa
3 1/2 tbsp (50 g) butter, melted
1/4 cup (25 g) chopped almonds
confectioners' (powdered) sugar for finishing

METHOD

Prepare the shortbread pastry. Mix the softened butter with the sugar, stir in a pinch of salt and the egg yolks. Add flour sifted with baking powder, cocoa and a pinch of vanilla powder, then knead briefly until you have a smooth, even paste. Wrap the dough in plastic wrap and leave to rest in the refrigerator for one hour. For the pastry cream, heat the milk in a saucepan with a quarter of a vanilla bean (cut open lengthways with a paring knife). Beat the egg yolk in a bowl with sugar, add the sifted flour and stir. Remove the vanilla bean from the milk. Pour a little boiling milk on the yolk, then gradually add the rest of the milk to temper it, whisking all the time. Put in a pan and bring to the boil. Dissolve the cocoa and chopped dark chocolate in the boiling cream. Pour into a bowl and leave to cool. On a floured surface, roll out 10 oz (300 g) of shortbread pastry with a rolling pin to a thickness of 1/8 in (3 mm). Line the bottom and sides of a buttered, floured cake tin. Keep the remaining dough to finish the cake. Spread 1/3 cup (80 ml) of the pastry cream on the bottom and arrange the washed, dried, and sliced peaches on it. Grind the almonds to a powder in a food processor and mix with the flour, starch, and cocoa powder, previously sifted together. In a bain-marie, lightly heat the eggs and yolks with the sugar, stirring with a whisk. Beat (preferably in a mixer), then gently incorporate the flour mixed with the other ingredients, stirring from the bottom up. Finally, stir in the warm, melted butter. Fill the cake tin three-quarters full and sprinkle with the chopped almonds. From the remaining dough, form two strips 1/10 in (2 mm) thick and 3/8–3/4-in (1 to 2-cm) wide. Arrange them on the cake, crossing one over the other. Bake at 350 °F (180 °C) for about 45 minutes. Leave to cool completely before removing from the mold, then sprinkle with confectioners' sugar.

Preparation time: 45' + 20' (shortbread pastry) + 25' (pastry cream) Cooking time: 45' Difficulty: high

CHOCOLATE AND PEAR GINGER TART

INGREDIENTS FOR 4/6 PEOPLE

For the shortbread pastry (the minimum quantity for good results)

1 1/4 cups (165 g) all-purpose flour
scant 1/2 cup (100 g) butter
generous 3/8 cup (85 g) sugar
1 egg
1/4 tsp (1 g) baking powder (optional)
vanilla powder
salt

For the filling

3 1/2 tbsp (50 g) butter
1/4 cup (50 g) sugar
1 egg
scant 1/3 cup (70 ml) milk
generous 3/4 cup (100 g) all-purpose flour
scant 1/4 cup (18 g) cocoa powder
2 tsp (5 g) baking powder
2 pears
fresh (or ground) ginger
salt

For finishing

1 3/4 oz (50 g) powdered gelatin for desserts
confectioners' (powdered) sugar

METHOD

Prepare the shortbread dough. Cream the softened butter with the sugar, then stir in a pinch of salt and the egg. Add the flour sifted with baking powder and pinch of vanilla powder and knead briefly until you have a smooth, even dough.
Wrap the dough in plastic wrap and leave to rest in the refrigerator for one hour.
On a floured surface, roll out 200 grams of dough with a rolling pin to a thickness of 1/8 in (3 mm). Line a buttered, floured cake tin.
Mix the butter and sugar in a bowl.
Combine the egg, milk, salt, and freshly grated ginger. Stir.
Stir in the sifted flour with the cocoa and baking powder (and ground ginger, if using).
Fill the cake tin lined with dough.
Peel the pears, cut them in half and remove the core, then slice them, not too finely.
Arrange the sliced pears on the cake, pressing down slightly.
Bake and cook at 340 °F (170 °C) for about 30 minutes.
Remove from the oven and leave to cool. Once the cake has cooled, brush some gelatin on the pears, then sprinkle everything with confectioners' (icing) sugar.

Preparation time: 30'
Cooking time: 30' Difficulty: medium

CHOCOLATE HAZELNUT CAKE

INGREDIENTS FOR **4/6** PEOPLE

For the cake
1/2 cup (125 g) butter
1 cup (125 g) confectioners' (powdered) sugar
4 1/2 tbsp (60 g) hazelnut paste
2 eggs + 1 egg yolk
1 cup (125 g) all-purpose flour
3 tbsp (15 g) cocoa
1 tsp (3 g) baking powder
vanilla powder

For the pasty cream (the minimum quantity for good results)
1/2 cup (125 ml) milk
1/4 vanilla bean
1 egg yolk
3 1/2 tbsp (40 g) sugar
4 tsp (10 g) all-purpose flour

For the gianduia cream
1/4 cup (65 ml) pastry cream
3/8 cup (85 g) butter
1/2 cup (50 g) confectioners' (powdered) sugar
3 tbsp (34 g) hazelnut paste
2 tsp (9 ml) liqueur to taste
6 tsp (8 g) cocoa
1 oz (25 g) dark chocolate

For the decoration
5 to 8 gianduiotti chocolates
chopped hazelnuts

METHOD

Work the softened butter and confectioners' (icing) sugar together in a bowl. Add the hazelnut paste and mix.
Stir in the eggs and yolk, then all the remaining ingredients sifted together.
Fill the buttered, floured cake tins three-quarters of the way to the top and bake in the oven at 350 °F (180 °C) for 30 minutes.
Remove from the oven and leave to cool.
For the pastry cream, heat 1/2 cup (125 ml) of milk in a saucepan with a quarter of a vanilla bean (cut open lengthways with a paring knife).
Remove the vanilla bean from the milk. In a bowl, beat the egg yolk with 3 1/2 tbsp (40 g) sugar, then add 4 tsp (10 g) all-purpose flour and stir.
Pour a little boiling milk on the yolk, then gradually add the rest of the milk to temper it. Put in a saucepan and cook until boiling.
For the hazelnut gianduia cream, take 1/4 cup (65 g) pastry cream and flavor it with cocoa and melted chocolate, preferably while still hot.
With a whisk, beat the softened butter and sugar in a bowl. Add the hazelnut paste and then the liqueur and flavored pastry cream. Beat the mixture again.
Divide the cake in half horizontally and spread one-third of the hazelnut gianduia cream on one of the halves.
Put the cake back together and cover it completely with the remaining hazelnut gianduia cream.
Add the chopped hazelnuts to the top of the cake, and decorate with the gianduiotti and the remaining cream.

Preparation time: 40' + 15' (gianduia cream)
Cooking time: 30' Difficulty: high

VIENNESE CAKE

INGREDIENTS FOR 4/6 PEOPLE

For the cake
3/4 cup (115 g) peeled, sweet almonds
1/10 oz (3 g) bitter almonds or apricot kernels
2/3 cup (137 g) sugar
3/8 cup (45 g) all-purpose flour
1 1/2 tbsp (12 g) potato starch
1/4 cup (25 g) cocoa powder
vanilla powder
salt
3 oz (82 g) dark chocolate
5 tsp (25 g) butter
5 egg yolks
4 egg whites

For the filling
4 oz (120 g) apricot jam
4 tsp (20 ml) orange liqueur

For the glaze
2/3 cup (170 ml) cream
5 tsp (25 ml) glucose syrup
6 oz (170 g) dark chocolate

METHOD

In a food processor, finely grind the almonds with 2 tbsp (25 g) of sugar, then mix in a bowl with the flour, starch, cocoa, vanilla, and a pinch of salt.
Melt the chocolate and butter together in bain-marie.
Separately, beat the yolks with 4 tbsp (50 g) of sugar and the egg whites with 1/3 cup (62 g) of sugar.
Lighten the beaten yolks with one-third of the beaten egg whites, then add the melted chocolate and butter.
Combine the mixture with the almonds, flour, starch, and cocoa.
Fold in the remaining egg whites.
Gently mix, using a soft spatula and stirring from the bottom up.
Pour into a greased, floured mold.
Bake at 350 °F (180 °C) for 40 to 45 minutes.
Remove from the oven, leave to cool, remove from the mold, and divide the cake into three layers, cut horizontally. Fill with apricot jam diluted in orange liqueur, and then spread more jam across the surface of the cake.
Chop the chocolate and place in a bowl. In a small saucepan, boil the cream with the glucose syrup and then pour it on the chocolate.
Stir with a wooden spoon until you have a smooth, velvety glaze with which to frost the cake.

Preparation time: 45'
Cooking time: 45' Difficulty: high

CHOCOLATE CUPCAKES WITH ORANGE AND BANANA

INGREDIENTS FOR 4/6 PEOPLE

3 1/2 tbsp (50 g) butter
1/4 cup (50 g) sugar
1 oz (30 g) dark chocolate
1 egg
1/4 cup (60 ml) milk
generous 3/4 cup (100 g) all-purpose flour
2 tbsp (10 g) cocoa powder
2 tsp (5 g) baking powder
1 orange
1 banana
salt

METHOD

Whip the softened butter and the sugar in a bowl with a whisk, then add the warm, melted chocolate.
Stir in the egg, milk, and a pinch of salt, and mix.
Stir in the sifted flour with the cocoa and baking powder.
Peel the banana and cut it into slices.
Peel the orange, then dice each individual segment.
Gently incorporate the fruit by stirring it into the mixture.
Fill buttered, floured single-serving molds.
Bake at 340 °F (170 °C) for about 20 minutes.
Remove from the oven and leave to cool.

Preparation time: 20'
Cooking time: 20' Difficulty: easy

SOFT-HEARTED CHOCOLATE CUPCAKES

INGREDIENTS FOR **4/6** PEOPLE

6 oz (180 g) dark chocolate
3 tbsp (40 g) butter
1/4 cup (50 g) sugar
generous 3/8 cup (50 g) all-purpose flour
5 egg whites
2 egg yolks

METHOD

In a saucepan, melt the dark chocolate and butter.
Meanwhile, in a bowl, whip the egg whites with a whisk.
When halfway done, add the sugar and continue until
you have a firm, snow-like substance.
Add the egg yolks to the egg whites and combine
with the melted chocolate and butter.
Delicately incorporate the sifted flour, stirring with a spatula
from the bottom up.
Pour into buttered, floured single-serve molds, three-quarters of the way up.
Store in the refrigerator or freezer.
When ready to serve, bake in the oven at 400 °F (200 °C)
for 5 to 6 minutes (8 to 10 minutes, if the cakes were frozen).
Serve immediately, so that the hearts of the cupcakes are still soft.

Preparation time: 20'
Cooking time: 5-10' Difficulty: medium

CHOCOLATE LOG

INGREDIENTS FOR 4/6 PEOPLE

For the chocolate rolls
1/2 cup (100 g) sugar
3 eggs
1 egg yolk
2/3 cup (80 g) all-purpose flour
2 1/2 tbsp (20 g) potato starch
3 tbsp (15 g) cocoa powder

*** the minimum quantity for good results**

For the pastry cream*
1/2 cup (125 ml) milk
1/4 vanilla bean
1 egg yolk
3 1/2 tbsp (40 g) sugar
4 tsp (10 g) all-purpose flour

For the chocolate butter cream
1/3 cup (85 g) pastry cream
1/2 cup (115 g) butter
1/2 cup (65 g) confectioners' (icing) sugar
1 tsp (5 g) hazelnut paste
1 tbsp (12 ml) liqueur to taste
2 tbsp (10 g) cocoa
1 oz (30 g) dark chocolate

For the syrup
2 tbsp (30 ml) water
generous 3/8 cup (80 g) sugar
2 1/2 tbsp (35 ml) rum

METHOD

For the chocolate rolls, sift the flour, starch, and cocoa together. Separate the eggs and beat the egg whites with the sugar. In another bowl, break up the egg yolks with a fork and fold them into the egg whites, then add the sifted flour and cocoa with starch. Spread a layer of dough about 3/8 in (1 cm) thick on a baking sheet lined with parchment paper. Bake at 450 °F (230° C) for 5 to 7 minutes.
For the pastry cream, heat 1/2 cup (125 ml) of milk in a saucepan with a quarter of a vanilla bean (cut open lengthways with a paring knife). In a bowl, beat the egg yolk with 3 1/2 tbsp (40 g) sugar, then add 4 tsp (10 g) all-purpose flour and stir. Remove the vanilla bean from the milk. Pour a little boiling milk on the yolk, then gradually add the rest of the milk to temper it. Put in a saucepan and bring to the boil.
For the chocolate butter cream, take 1/3 cup (85 ml) of pastry cream and flavor it, preferably while still hot, with the cocoa and melted chocolate. In a bowl, beat the softened butter and sugar with a whisk. Add the hazelnut paste, then the liqueur and flavored pastry cream. Beat everything again.
For the rum syrup, boil the sugar and water together, let it cool, and then add the liqueur.
Place the dough on a sheet of parchment paper and drench it with the syrup. With a spatula, spread one-third to one-half of the cream and roll the cake, using the paper to help the process.
Let stand in the refrigerator for half an hour.
Finish the log by covering it with the remaining butter cream, using a piping bag with a notched piping tip.

Preparation time: 15' + 25' (dough for chocolate roll) + 10' (butter and chocolate cream) + 10' (syrup)
Resting time: 30' Difficulty: easy

ALPHABETICAL INDEX OF RECIPES

ALPHABETICAL INDEX OF INGREDIENTS

All the photographs are by Academia Barilla except:

123RF: pages 2, 4-5, 7, 9, 10
Biwa Studio/Getty Images: pages 12-13, 30-31, 44-45, 70-71, 82-83, 98-99
Private collection: pages 14, 16, 18, 20, 22, 24, 26, 28, 32, 34, 36, 38, 40, 42, 46, 48, 50, 52, 54, 56, 58, 60, 62, 64, 66, 68, 72, 74, 76, 78, 80, 84, 86, 88, 90, 92, 94, 96, 100, 102, 104, 106, 108, 110, 112, 114, 116, 118, 120, 122

ACADEMIA BARILLA

AMBASSADOR OF ITALIAN CUISINE IN THE WORLD

In the heart of Parma, recognized as one of the most prestigious capitals of cuisine, the Barilla Center stands in the middle of Barilla's historical headquarters, now hosting Academia Barilla's modern structure. Founded in 2004 with the aim of affirming the role of Italian culinary arts, protecting the regional gastronomic heritage, defending it from imitations and counterfeits and to valorize the great tradition of Italian cooking, Academia Barilla is where great professionalism and unique competences in the world of cuisine meet. The institution organizes cooking courses for those passionate about food culture, offering services dedicated to the operators in the sector and proposing products of unparalleled quality. Academia Barilla was awarded the "Business-Culture Prize" for its promotional activities regarding gastronomic culture and Italian creativity in the world.
The headquarters were designed to meet the educational needs in the field of food preparation and have the multimedia tools necessary to host large events: around an extraordinary gastronomic auditorium, there are an internal restaurant, a multisensory laboratory and various classrooms equipped with the most modern technology. In the Gastronomic Library are conserved over 12,000 volumes regarding specific topics and an unusual collection of historical menus and printed materials on the culinary arts: the library's enormous cultural heritage is available online and allows anyone to access hundreds of digitalized historical texts. This forward thinking organization and the presence of an internationally renowned team of professors guarantee a wide rage of courses, able to satisfy the needs of both catering professionals as well as simple cuisine enthusiasts. Academia Barilla also organizes cultural events and initiatives for highlighting culinary sciences open to the public, with the participation of experts, chefs and food critics. Since 2012 Academia Barilla has been organizing the Pasta World Championship, in which chefs from all around the world are participating.

www.academiabarilla.com

WHITE STAR PUBLISHERS

WS White Star Publishers® is a registered trademark
property of De Agostini Libri S.p.A.

Via G. da Verrazano, 15 - 28100 Novara, Italy
www.whitestar.it - www.deagostini.it

Translation: Salvatore Ciolfi
Editing: Rosetta Translations SARL

ISBN 978-88-544-0667-4
5 6 7 8 20 19 18 17 16

Printed in China